Painted Souls

Also by Barbara Olds and published by Ginninderra Press
Boundary Rider
My Walk with the Black Dog (Pocket People)

Barbara Olds

Painted Souls

Painted Souls
ISBN 978 1 74027 851 5
Copyright © text Barbara Olds 2014
Cover image © queen21 – fotolia.com

First published 2014
Reprinted 2017

Ginninderra Press
PO Box 3461 Port Adelaide SA 5015
www.ginninderrapress.com.au

Contents

Painted Souls	7
Crayola Crayons	9
Apples	10
Backyard Igloo	12
Dolls	13
Morsels of Memory	15
Once upon a time…	17
Stevie Whittaker	18
Batter Up	19
Photographs	21
First Aussie Christmas	22
At the Illawarra Fly	24
Boat Ride	25
Cook Strait	26
The Rockies	27
Ice-bound	28
Esplanade	30
Peace Park	31
Touching History	32
South China Sea	34
An Asian Landscape	35
Tiananmen Square 2007	36
Reflections on China	37
Thien Cung Caves	38
Handbag Heaven	39
Nympheas	40
Parisian Tapestry	41
Dabbling	45
Some Days	46
Painted Rocks	47

Clutter	48
In the Gutter	49
Seaside	50
Predator	51
Snake	52
Reflection	53
Remembrance	54
Fresh Powder	55
Fog-bound	56
Breathless	58
Facial	59
Featherlight	60
Flame	61
Friday Night at Vascos	62
Let There Be Spirits	63
Concrete	64
Lingering	65
Goodbye…and again	66
Nasturtiums	67
Seeking Saluan	69
Shadows	70
Siren Sea	71
Still Standing	72
Stranger in the Night	73
What Shade the Purple Heart?	76
Windblown	77
Word-bound	78
Unbound	79

Painted Souls

The ghosts of our lives
Sail ships through our history
Magically shaping our character

Will we choose to live
In the catacombs of that history
Or the cathedrals of the future
What pieces go together
To make our masks

Our window on the world
Shattered one moment
Re-fused the next with
Coloured glass
Backlit and stained

The icons of our youth
Tempted us
With new ways to live
And we answered with
Desire and abandon

We call on magic
And sleight of hand
To fit the occasions
Of our lives

Our character
Crafted by our
Internal artisan
Weaving the threads
Dyed by life

We wear our masks
To protect our souls
Painted as they are
By the splash
Of cultural colour
And the indelible ink
Of experience

Crayola Crayons

Green and yellow
the joy of the box of 64
fresh and new
each crayon pointing
upwards, reaching
for the sky

A box of imagination
and unlimited possibility
even before the first mark
is put upon the blank page
with names that take you
away into dreams

I remember the sound
of the colours as they rolled
off my tongue
my favourites
burnt sienna
indigo blue

The colours follow me
blending together
the powders of
culture and mood
the grounding earth
the night sky
the cobbled streets of Italy
the *shibori* dyes of Japan

They are the essence
of my life's colouring book

Apples

1

Isaac Newton sits quietly
beneath the apple tree when,
suddenly, a ripened apple falls
and in a moment of serendipity
he 'discovers' gravity

2

The apple of his eye
blonde and blue-eyed
bouncing about, twisting
him round her finger
'Daddy, come see what I've made'
he attends her call and finds
to his wonder
a five-storey house of cards

3

Times Square
the Big Apple's core
bustles, especially at night,
hawkers for clubs promise
big-busted women
scantily clad while
at the legitimate theatres
limousines disgorge
the well-heeled as
others arrive by
horse-drawn carriage
half-price ticket-holders
look on in reverence
or disdain

4

He cuts two apples
halved then quartered
the core cut away
the sections of each
placed on the plate
Sorrento by Mikasa
eight sections curved
around the rim, left and right
he calls from the kitchen
'The apples are cut'

Backyard Igloo

With willowy hands and
a bare steel blade
my father carved four slabs
of crystallised snow from our yard.

Carefully he placed the slabs
against a tenuous wooden frame
that was nestled between
two tall pine trees.

A piece of fabric, rescued
and recycled
hung at the opening
through which I struggled.

Protected from the winter wind
I sat in that igloo
made for me
by my champion.

Dolls

When I was young
My father travelled
And when he came home
He would bring me presents
Music boxes, Mikimoto pearls
And dolls

The Dutch dolls were
Robust and sturdy
The boy from Volendam
Cloth face and body
Felt clothes and wooden clogs
A pipe that broke years ago

The girl, pretty
In her printed dress,
Starched white pinafore
Arms made of 1950s plastic

They stood side by side
On my window sill, sparkling
Blonde in the sun
Until her arms softened and
Became long, dry and cracked
Old woman arms

From Argentina
Came the gaucho
And his lady

He, bearded, in native costume
His hat jauntily positioned
Bolo at the ready
She in cotton polka dots
Her long dark hair plaited
Perhaps, not his lady
After all

And then
There was the geisha
Dancing
Silken red kimono
Gold threads entwined
Her black hair upswept
Pale nape revealed
Sensual
Still

Morsels of Memory

I tugged on Inez's apron
and was rewarded with tidbits
and surprised looks
as I chomped away
on raw onion

Birthday doughnuts
from Colonial Bakery
with a gaggle of girls
after swimming and
before the celebratory slumber

Toasting marshmallows
over the open flame
to be eaten squished
between Hershey chocolate
and the crunch of graham crackers

Ben's Restaurant for pastrami
hot on rye with mustard
or boiled in sealed packets
by Koorsh, of course
pastrami heaven at home

Sara Lee banana cake
half frozen
eaten in secret
in the basement
as I watch late-night TV

Submarine sandwiches
from the shop in North Conway
until the local takeaway
complained
and got exclusive rights

Hofbrau spaghetti
and buckets of stuffing
a sobering carb overload
to quell 2 a.m. munchies
and absorb hours of alcohol

Once upon a time…

her nimble fingers
plied the needle
and crimped the crusts
of countless apple pies

fashioned silk ribbons
into bows and
tinkled the ivories
music merry making

held pen to paper
scratching and
rat-a-tatted keys
sending memories
to friends and lovers

made fists and firmly
gripped the racquet
smashing volleys
hard cross court

once upon a time…

but no longer

Stevie Whittaker

I loved Stevie Whittaker

He was an older man,
his first grade to my kindy.

Each afternoon I waited
for the school bus to arrive
and for him to alight.

Several times a week
we married
in his basement.

For Christmas
he got a cowboy hat,
a silver star and a holster
with two six-shooters.

'Reach for the sky'
he would shout
as he challenged passersby.

That summer
my family moved away
and we lost touch.

Now, I watch him
in home movies,
brandishing those guns
and wonder…

Did he reach the sky?

Batter Up

Tie score
bottom of the ninth
two outs.

The batter stands square to the plate
the bat over his right shoulder
elbows raised, ready.

The pitcher stares into the catcher's mitt,
quickly squints to read the signs,
and shakes his head, 'No.'
Another set of signs,
another negative shake.

The batter straightens
and steps out of the box.
He taps his feet with the bat
the left, then the right
tap tap, tap tap.
He takes a few practice swings
before stepping back into the box
and assuming the position.

This time, the pitcher
nods to the catcher and
accepts the sign.

He readies himself
swings his arm back and
lets the ball fly.
It whirls over the plate
just inside the corner.

The batter stands still and
the umpire shouts 'Strike one.'

The catcher tosses back the ball
the pitcher readies himself again
and delivers, this time a fast ball.

The batter swings but
the ball swirls past before
he can connect.
'Strike two.'

Now confident he can
get this last out
to force extra innings,
the pitcher takes a moment,
collects his thoughts and
nods assuredly to the catcher.

Again,
the wind-up
the release
the delivery of the ball.

The crack of bat on ball
resounds throughout the park and,
as the ball sails over the fence,
the batter begins his
round of the bases.

Game over.

Photographs

families exposed…

the true
the false

I see the smiles
but wonder
what lies beneath

whose eyes are mine
whose smile
where is the truth
of my creation

where was my photograph
developed…

families exposed

First Aussie Christmas

'Twas Christmas in the city
We planned to celebrate
On arrival it was hot and dry
The Celsius, thirty-eight

The rellies they did drop by
In long drawn-out procession
To be greeted and seated
Each one in swift succession

So many new names and faces
For me to contemplate
Could I remember them all
Or would I be fish bait?

They wanted to see
Who Kevin had brought home
Now, would I pass muster
Or leave all alone?

Like a fish out of water
I tried to fit in
People they did roam about
My head was in a spin

Gathered at the table
Chaos lay ahead
They were grabbing here and there
Lord, I wish I was dead

By Christmas Day dinner
It was one over forty
Hot turkey and ham
Roast veg, oh Lordy!

Of pickled pork and pudding
We all had our fill
Let's waddle to the lounge room
Please, O stomach, be still

There were presents for everyone
My only gifts were for Kevin
But they'd bought me presents
Had I found Christmas heaven?

I survived the whole day
Why had I been fretting?
No obstacles now
Let's plan the wedding

The day soon arrived
For us to depart
We said our goodbyes
Phew, I'm in their hearts

Yes, it is Christmas in the city
We celebrate still
What city, you ask?
Why, where else…Broken Hill

At the Illawarra Fly

on steel walkways
suspended
the vibrations testing
my resolve
we traverse the treetops

green slivers of eucalypt
blossoms white in anticipation
of the honeybees' buzz
tree fern shadows on the path
in negative image

there is haze towards the sea
but the spits of land and stacks
of Port Kembla are clear
while, in the undergrowth,
the rustle of an elusive lyrebird
brings me back to the natural world

on our drive back
my first snake in the wild
as it coils
and lunges
across the warm blacktop

Boat Ride

Silent
Except for
The rhythmic slap
Of wave on bow
Lost in thoughts
And memories

Moving through the sea
Timeless skies
Endless breezes
And glistening moonlight
Accompany me
Day to night
Night to day

Cook Strait

MS *Volendam*

We sail on a south-easterly track.
Now the cloud mist
that earlier obscured Mount Taranaki
surrounds our ship,
dulling the sharpness
of the maritime lights.

The orange of a passing vessel
the blinking of a buoy
the marker of some
close-to-shore menace.
Directly above, even
the single star sports a halo.

Below, the inked sea is broken
by our white foam wake,
while pale-winged birds
skim the water. Why at night
when they should be away
huddled in their nests?

Hour by hour we sail on,
our destination known.
But our journey proceeds
at the whim
of the sea
and the siren.

The Rockies

Mountains that soar
always capped
in snow, never
bare to the sun

Long ago
they forced
their way
shattered
the earth's crust
and, even now,
continue their
climb to
the sky
majestic
in their presence

Unflappable
Untamed
Unforgiving
Unforgettable

Ice-bound

Early this morning
the ice drifted by
leisurely, bobbing
in the ship's wake.

But our pace
has slowed, barely two knots,
and the ice isn't drifting
no longer is there floe.

The ice is packed
an irregular mosaic,
with grout lines narrowed
and shapes offset.

The crunch as our ship moves on
punctuates the stillness
the fear of being trapped
descends upon me.

If we continue
will the floe meld together
an immovable
sheet of white?

Word from the bridge,
we turn back,
behind us a wide arc
our wake only briefly free of ice.

Slowly, we edge out
of the Okhotsk Sea
back to the Sea of Japan
and head south.

Later, at Sitka,
when we tender to the shore,
will we see bare metal at the bow
scraped clean of its layers of paint,
gleaming from its close
encounter with the ice?

Esplanade

At Nagasaki
along the waterfront
away from the pier
stretches
an esplanade of peace
where paved spaces
wend their way
along the man-made canal

We cross a grassy knoll and find
a cascading stream, fed
by a timely geyser,
erupting and sending
rhythmic waves of water,
tumbling along,
caressing the stream's stone bed,
a crescendo at the final drop
and then,
as the geyser recedes,
the water becomes gentle,
pianissimo,
a calm whisper

Peace Park

The broad path leads
past the remnants
of a prison's stone foundation
into an expanse of
other nations' regret.

In the distance
colourful banners
attract the eye
and outline
the giant bronze-patina
man-god
pointing the way to
peace and,
perhaps,
understanding.

Here at the point
beneath Ground Zero
a place to contemplate
and remember.

Touching History

past the mounted photos
enlarged to show the devastation

past the mock up
of Fat Man
into the room
within which
glass cases hold
the artefacts of that
explosion

I wonder at it all
and nod, agreeing with
the commentary, duly contrite
for a generation's decision

when
one highlighted case
draws my attention

there, not under glass,
but out
in the open
the misshapen remains
of a bottle

there to touch
to feel
knowing you are
in the presence of
a being, which,
as inanimate as it seems,
is a survivor,
a reminder of the day

as my fingers glide over
its smooth green surface
I feel history
as never before

South China Sea

the moon,
cloud-shrouded
and near-full,
lies off our starboard side

the horizon separates
the grey of the sky
and the black of the sea
while along its line

lights, in twos and threes,
sparkle
perhaps boats or buoys
or islands unknown

beyond them
dimmer lights,
mere pinpricks,
I imagine to be the shore

An Asian Landscape

Tenement facades
but what lies within

Laundry on poles horizontally
placed, row by row
on the balcony
balcony by balcony

Air conditioner units hang
and I fear a wayward
pigeon's weight will
topple them to the
streets below

Water has stained the walls
long streaks, thin fingers
from the roof to the bustle
of the street

But within the walls
curtains, too large for their windows,
billow, not from the wind,
but from within

What secrets would I find
if I could see beyond those walls

Would I find the chaos
of the streets
or an ordered and pristine
world of reverence

Tiananmen Square 2007

The square is bounded
by the Hall of the People
Mao's Mausoleum
the Forbidden City
and a museum, now clad
in a façade that counts the days,
hours and minutes until
Beijing's big party for the world.

The once contentious square,
no longer filled by tanks
and that lone protestor,
overflows with sightseers from
both in and out of China.

The marching sections
of green men are
a sight
of interest,
not menace.

A small boy revels
in his tuxedo-clad splendour
a youthful adjunct to a wedding
while an elderly Chinese woman
approaches, not to ask our help
in taking her family's photo,
but to entice us
to be photographed with her.

Westerners in her world.

Reflections on China

My ears echo
with the clamour of
'one dollar, one dollar'
as my mind tries to fathom
the chaos that is China

What lottery decides
the randomness
of tearing down and building up
the bamboo scaffolding
and the modern iron
as workers shine lights 24/7

Tall 'modern' apartment buildings
with individual satellite dishes
and clothes hanging on balconies
in old and new parts of town

The attitudes of fellow travellers
surprised that I would eat with chopsticks
a cacophony of sights, sounds, smells and people
the twig brooms used by street sweepers
from the Maglev a view
over market gardens
blue roofs and canals

The dichotomy of old and new China
a country drawn
kicking and screaming
into the twenty-first century

Thien Cung Caves

We travel through
the green slate water
of Halong Bay
our boat making ripples
as we pass erupted hillocks
each one a testament to nature

We are headed to
the rainbow caves
of Thien Cung
heritage listed
picturesque
in their simplicity

Static now, no longer growing
their stalactites or stalagmites
there is permanence
in the figures of
elephant and maiden
set for time immemorial

Lit by coloured globes
shadows appear as never before
with only a fleeting
glimpse of natural light
filtering from above

Handbag Heaven

As a child
I sought out
small spaces
where I withdrew
into my own world
taking with me
my thoughts
my treasures

Now grown and
no longer fit
for small spaces
I put my world
into the most common
of all locales
my handbag

At Takashimaya
in Singapore
an entire floor is
dedicated to a wondrous
array of that keeper of treasures

And there
in handbag heaven
I 'ooh' and 'aah'
and imagine
the bliss
my world could be

Nympheas

What was I?
fourteen, perhaps,
when I saw my first
Monet – water lilies –
adorning the chimney breast
of a friend's home.

Love at first sight.

It would be years
before I saw them again
in multitude
first,
in New York
and then,
in reverence,
in Paris
in abundance.

Close in the brush strokes
thick and thin, colours
meshed and layered
discernible as individual
spots but, in adding distance
from the canvas,
the strokes came into focus and
what appeared as random
morphed into the magic
that is Monet.

Parisian Tapestry

The Paris of my dreams
was woven from
the films of my youth
the songs of Françoise Hardy
and the paintings of Monet.

But travelling there
challenged my *vie en rose*
with its reality.

That first midnight, moonlit
with a breeze
that caught the scent
of spring
and brought it to me
as tourists gazed at
the hourly illumination
that is the Eiffel Tower.

By day, I wondered
at the expanse of Paris
as I watched from its highest platform
while terror struck as I descended
the ironwork staircase that clung
to one tower leg
splaying ever outward.

At the Palais Royale
the columns of the Colonnade
let me imagine Audrey Hepburn
running, chased by
a villainous Walter Matthau.
In the gardens an old man
sat reading while, from
his cupped right hand,
sparrows fed on birdseed.

On the *bateau mouche*
I sensed Cary Grant
as he and Audrey shared
a meal and a confession.
Voices echoed as they
passed under stone bridges,
spotlights on Notre-Dame.

I struggled to see those sights
through the scratched and faded windows
of my *bateau* and realised
once back on land
the stunning photos
of Notre-Dame's arches
were snapped from the back.

The genius of the
multi-level labyrinth
that is the Metro
impressed with its efficiency and
pulsated with the energy of Paris
while the stench of urine
also revealed it
as a home for vagrants.

The funicular,
quaint and picturesque,
was jammed with disciples
headed to the re-enactment
of Jesus carrying the cross
in the shadow of
a pristine Sacré-Coeur,
the sunlight reflected
by its white dome
negating the need for flash.

Nearby, Montmartre bustled
as artists charged highly
for their wares and, on occasion,
tempted tourists to an evening rendezvous
in hopes of making a bigger sale.
While sidewalk cafés,
replete with locals and tourists
and the ever-present pampered pooches,
added to the atmosphere
and teased the senses
with the fragrance of French onion soup
and an array of patisserie delights.

And through it all
drumming in my head
Françoise sang, reminding me
of the romance of Paris
the hand-in-hand of *tous les garçons et filles*.

Now my Paris
is woven from the romance of the past
the sights and sounds of the city
and the realities of
joy and sorrow
wonder and fear
light and shadow.

Dabbling

I've spent my life
dabbling
a bit of this
a bit of that
touching the surface
of each new thing
but…
I get bored
before committing myself
and becoming
so entrenched
there's no escaping
the quagmire
of being
an expert

Some Days

There are days when I feel dull

When I realise I'll never
paint like Picasso
or sing like Sarah Vaughan

Computers only confuse
and foreign policy leaves me lost

I don't understand football and,
except for turning the ignition key,
how my car works is a mystery

Convincing the teacher why
Hamlet acted as he did or
how the Franco-Prussian War
affected the modern make-up
of Europe are beyond me

But I can string
a row of words together
capture a memory
and create a song

Painted Rocks

I painted rocks today

Rocks that eons ago
Spewed from volcanoes
Scattered and wound
Their way to BC's shore
Water-tempered to smooth

With pick and pencil
Dots of sizes various
Appeared
Colours overlaid
One upon the other
In patterns
Pulled from the ether
Reflected in the surrounding sea

Lacquered into permanence
I now cradle the dotted rocks
In the palm of my hand
As worry beads
They bring memories
And comfort

Clutter

This room is messy
overflowing with files
and filled with piles
of projects,
unfinished

When the cleaner comes today
she will edge her way
around the piles
as the vacuum deftly sucks
bits of fabric and
scraps of paper torn
in dismay
at the words they hold

When I return
the smell of lemon
will assail my senses,
a cleansing smell,
the room refreshed
and energised

In the Gutter

I nearly missed it as I crossed the road

There, in the gutter,
dirty red, half-covered
by fallen leaves
torn asunder
by the relentless rains
of our non-summer

Its pointed end
aimed straight at me
a seed pod
or dried chilli, perhaps

No,
a scrap of leather, shaped
a narrow shoe

Somewhere a doll goes barefoot

Seaside

A solitary gull flies
Silhouette against the sky
Its wing tip caressing
The ocean's crest

Water races to the sand
Only to retreat
As if it had no right
To bathe in the bright of day

Passersby collect shells
Broken by the waves
And carry them off
For days of 'remember when'

Predator

The hawk soars amidst the clouds
then plummets endlessly
to hunt a prey that
grovels in the sands
darting from rock to ledge
and shadow to shadow

Coming closer, the claws
pierce his small prey
and, with eyes wild with desire,
the hawk anticipates the kill,
as eager claws tear,
instinctively,
the beak ripping flesh from bone
the wine red life seeping
from that which it has claimed,
the prize won

Within the killer's clawed grasp
the heart, no longer beating,
the carcass lying still
bloodied sands drying
beneath the burning sun
and the hawk
soaring high,
triumphant

Snake

Have you seen
drops of venom
falling – milked
or the snake's tongue
flicker as it smells
your presence

Have you felt
his mosaic scales
diamond-shaped
and smooth

Have you seen
the last of a white
mouse's tail and
the bulge
it later becomes

Have you felt
the strength of
the snake
as you held him
round your shoulders

Have you seen
the path of a sidewinder or
the flare of the cobra's hood
or his power as he lunges
at the charmer

Reflection

Yesterday
the old woman
gazed upon her garden
a world of her making
a statement of her being.

The love and care
of choice and chance,
colour and creation.

Now that world
is cast aside
drowned by the weather.

The old woman wonders,
if her creation
has vanished from view,
does she still exist?

Remembrance

Theirs had been the great war.

Old souls,
suspended in time,
reliving the battles
they'd fought on foreign soil.

Lost comrades remembered,
friends they'd found
in the pain of war
still held in their hearts.

The last two,
standing together,
in remembrance
of the fallen.

If they'd known
it wouldn't be the last,
would they have been so willing
to die for the cause?

And what of our newest comrades,
how will the future
remember them as they return
from far-off deserts
to our golden shores?

Will we think of you
as heroes or villains?
How will your garden grow?

Fresh Powder

The mountain drew him
The powder
Natural not man-made
A delicate sparkling coat
Over sculpted slopes

From the top
He could see for miles
See the run for the challenge it was

He was in his element
That heavenly place
Where crisp cold air
Would rush against his skin
As he plummeted down

With his days of times and finishes gone
And medals no longer part of his life
This was as close to the feel
Of the race as he could get
The sharp edge of his skis
Making tracks, powder flying
At each sharp turn

The fresh powder
As it always did
Took him back to
The thrill of the chase

Fog-bound

When at sea
the mournful sound
of a warning horn
repeats
and repeats
searching for an echo

In Canberra
on a winter's morning
the fog rolls in early
to envelop the landscape
and when the sun burns through
the hilltops are visible
but the valleys are still shrouded
a mist bubbling up
from the ground
fingers following
the rivers and creeks

In the San Joaquin Delta
thick tule fog hugs the ground
even if clear crisp skies are above
when driving
forget the high beams
they send back
a sheet of glare
that blinds you
more than the fog

At times I find myself
living in the fog
the grey place
between clarity
and obscurity
the obvious
and the mysterious

And then
quick as a flash
the fog lifts
the path is
crystal clear
there, just waiting for me
to take that first step

Breathless

The air of morning,
a winter's morning,
with mouthed steam
as I walk and exhale

Then, the moment
of inhalation
when cold air
seeps into my lungs
making them spasm

Leaving me…
breathless

Facial

languid soothing strokes
the heat of hands
melting

the tap tap of fingers
percussion beats
invigorating

the smell of cucumber
my eyes rejoice
cooling

Featherlight

She draped
Her long black tresses
Over his body
It was as if he was touched
By the gentlest of breezes

Sensation
Shivers
Desire

Back and forth
Her head moved
With her face covered
By this black curtain
She felt free

Flame

A flickering flame
casts its hypnotising trance
as dripping tears of wax
add to a melting pool of thought
Farther my mind travels into
the translucent realm of being
until…
a gust of reality passes by
and extinguishes
the flickering flame
of perhaps

Friday Night at Vascos

A ballet of glasses, bottles and plates
as waiters twist and turn
midst the tables

An effortless choreography
punctuated by the swish swish of
steaming milk

A Mexican wave of laughter
flows over me as I enjoy
the camaraderie of my companions

After capturing the moment
in my mind
I move on

Let There Be Spirits

Let there be Spirits,
Guardian Spirits,
around me.

I watch John Edward
trying, almost desperately,
to convince myself
that my birth parents
watch over me.

I like to think of them
as together
and that they know
that I am here
and that I know of them.

I want a sign!
Give me a sign!
Isn't there something
that will let me know?

My daddy's here
with me
I sense him
Near.

They never knew me…
what I looked like,
the person I was.

How would they find me now?
If they look in the 'cosmos'
over Michigan,
they'll never find me.

Concrete

I'm in
You're out
Concrete divides us

I can hear you
There, on your side,
Nails scratching

As your fingers claw
The roughened surface
The mottled grey
Harbours traces
Of your DNA

Much as I want to risk it
My heart needs protection
So, in this case,
Concrete means survival

Lingering

The familiarity of my grief
Comforts me

Warm in its shroud
There are no thoughts
Of future

I hear only sounds
Swirling, buzzing
Urging, advising, admonishing

Still,
I linger

Goodbye…and again

When death is imminent
the mind is filled
with the person
who is dying

The memories of the past
flood into the conscious mind
overwhelming emotion sees
tears well in the eyes

Its imminence is
all-consuming and
each death is amplified
by memories of previous deaths
and allows us to grieve again
for those who have gone before

Nasturtiums

On living in the shade

They would linger
In the midst of their day
Pausing briefly to catch their breath

I scattered around them
Between the leaves of the oak
Dappling the ground with my cover

Yesterday, She sat with me
In the pale wicker chair
Her eyes gently closed, listening
The Girl brought the small tray
Placing it on the blue cloth
That covers the table
He brought from Portugal

She loves the table
But the cloth
Makes it more genteel

On the tray
Pale yellow pears
And soft creamy cheese
Next to slices of warm dark bread
And small round cakes
Topped with pink icing

I mingle in the sights
And smells
And remember other such days
When They sat with me

Alone now
She keeps the tradition alive
Each Saturday,
Sitting, eating the foods He loved

On occasions
When the wind blows gently
And the dapple catches her eye
She speaks to Him
Of how the children have grown
And moved away
How the house is too large
For only the Girl and She

Late in the afternoon,
Tired by the warmth of the day
She sleeps

The Girl takes the tray
And covers Her with a shawl
She is at peace

Seeking Saluan

across the rippled waters
moonlight danced,
sparkling, on point

quietly I sat
watching, waiting
for a signal from the sea

one flash
for success
two, I start again

at the sight of the lamplight
into the sea
I slid my canoe

paddling slowly
carefully silent
I reached my goal

there, from the depths,
emanated the glow
of gold

highlighted by the lamp
the mythic creature
rose and reared

breaking the surface
free from the water's hold
coming up, reborn

I had found
the treasure at last
my Goddess, Saluan

Shadows

Shadows dance
as flames lick the air
warming the cool night
and our huddled bodies

The light in a sea
of black on black
letting loose sparkles
that rise high into the sky

We watch until they join
a myriad of stars
more than we've seen before
with our big city eyes

There in the dry creek bed
we see shooting stars
lace paths of light
that our dreams can follow

Siren Sea

The Lorelei rock towers over us
as we cruise the Rhine, but
in daylight there is no magic in her voice
no call for me to abandon the safety of our ship

But one night on a distant ocean
with the dark silhouette of Cuba
to our starboard, warm breezes wafting
the moon lighting her way

The siren calls to me
from below the white webs of froth
and foam, the dark sea broken by our bow
dispersed in ever-changing patterns
magic to my eyes

Lost in the dance of the sea,
her call is amplified
So inviting the siren song
So haunting in its melody
So hard to resist

Still Standing

for Dr Lou

I loved Lou
he said it was transference
and I'm sure he was right
but I still loved him

he was there from the onset
through the rants and raves
the babbling
the interventions – drug-induced and more
the fleeting moments of hope

he saw the flaws and
the facets of my mind
and kept the faith

and when, at long last,
the rants decreased
the babbling stopped
and the moments of hope
less fleeting
he set me free

and now, forty years on,
I'm still standing

Stranger in the Night

A humid summer night
I was restless and sleep eluded me
But the crisp crack of glass
Brought me back from the brink
To the dark of an unlit house
Muffled voices, distant or near?
And a dark silhouette
Against the bedroom door

The stranger stood
No answers to my questions
Of who and what and why
Just steps taken forward
Till he sat, too close,
On the side of the bed
Its already narrow width
Overpowered by his bulk

The smell of his sweat
Mixed with the sickly
Sweet of liquor
'I make my own doors'
He proffered

At thirteen
I knew enough to be afraid
'Go away, I won't tell
They don't have to know
You were here'

Captive, mind panicking
I muster a shout
The hall light flicks on
And draws him out
Safe, but for how long

My father and the man
Confront each other
Boxers in the ring
Judging the other's prowess
Readying themselves for the fight
And then, in a blink,
He's back
Straight to the window
To find his friends

No, not more of them,
Please, no
We'll be outnumbered

From the corner of my eye
Movement
Two more men
Them?
No, no, I'm safe again

The police take him away
And still my questions
Unanswered
Who and what and why

The testimony, an affidavit
Nolo contendere, no contest
But if it happens again…
He was saved from prison
But not I

I have forgotten his name
But not the fear

What Shade the Purple Heart?

Are there degrees of purple
for the pains inflicted
by senseless acts

Should my pain deserve
a darker heart
in recompense
for it is ongoing
while yours
a moment's ache

But there are no purple hearts
for the pains we suffer
Just bruises
to ourselves
and our souls

Windblown

Leaves cover the grass
Scattered like
So many yesterdays

        Forgotten

While skies fill
With windblown
Tomorrows

        Hoped

Word-bound

Where are the words
that only weeks ago
spilled so easily
upon the page

Black shapes on white paper
line by line
the thoughts
the feelings
reflections of experience
echoes of life

They have escaped
gone back to their
hiding place
in the unreachable
depths of my mind

Unbound

No longer tied
to the past, free
from its restraint
no longer held

My mind soars
to new heights
grabs at life and
shares the experience

With words
hammered smooth
forming pictures
of life unbound

www.ingramcontent.com/pod-product-compliance
Lightning Source LLC
Chambersburg PA
CBHW062149100526
44589CB00014B/1757